AMERICAN BUSBOY

D1515005

AKRON SERIES IN POETRY

Titles published since 2003.
For a complete listing of titles published in the
series, go to www.uakron.edu/uapress/poetry

AMERICAN BUSBOY

MATTHEW GUENETTE

The University of Akron Press
Akron, Ohio

15   14   13   12   11   5   4   3   2   1

LIBRARY OF CONGRESS CATALOGING-IN-PUBLICATION DATA
Guenette, Matthew, 1972–
American busboy : poems / by Matthew Guenette.
    p. cm. — (Akron series in poetry)
ISBN 978-1-931968-98-0 (cloth : alk. paper) — ISBN 978-1-931968-97-3 (pbk. : alk. paper)
I. Title.
PS 3607. U 45A 84 2011
811'.6—DC 22
                          2011008197

The paper used in this publication meets the minimum requirements of ANSI / NISO Z 3 9 . 4 8–
1992 (Permanence of Paper). ∞

Cover: With Butter, by Matthew Guenette, copyright © 2010. Used with permission. Cover
design: Amy Freels

American Busboy was designed and typeset by Amy Freels in Joanna MT, with Sign Painter display.
American Busboy was printed on sixty-pound natural and bound by BookMasters of Ashland, Ohio.

ACKNOWLEDGMENTS

Special thanks to the following journals where versions of these poems have appeared: The
Associative Press, Barn Owl Review, Crab Creek Review, Cream City Review, diode, Evergreen Review, Interim, The
National Poetry Review, The New Anonymous, The New Orleans Review, Pindeldyboz, Toronto Quarterly, Umbrella, and
Southern Indiana Review.

To everyone in the Parlour (Denver, D.C., you know who you are), Jay Robinson for the endless
support, Kate Jenkins for wise revisions, the Hessen-Wisconsin Literary Fellowship, Rebecca
Stafford and all the MadCity Poets, Adrian Matejka and Stacey Lynn Brown, my incredible teach-
ers: Allison Joseph, Lucia Perillo, Rodney Jones ...

To my brothers, and my brothers: Josh Bell, Ron Mitchell, Michael Theune ...

To everyone at the University of Akron Press that helped bring this book into being, especially
the amazing Amy Freels, for vision and patience ...

And to Mary Biddinger: I will always be grateful ...

For Jules, August, and Josephine...

CONTENTS ....

THE CLAM SHACK!

THE CLAM SHACK!

—PROLOGUE—

for Josh Bell

When we failed to steal lobsters
from a rival's tank
they made us eat
fistfuls of tartar sauce.

Busing tables
is a form of worship—
The managers would be screaming—
BUSING TABLES

IS A FORM OF WORSHIP!
until we became abstract compositions,
shocked into prepping
the Golden-Brown Traps

for whatever the hell
Golden-Brown Traps prepared.
On Labor Day
they pierced our nipples

for The Monster Triple Shifts,
made us understand
our loved ones
would never understand

but the training held
certain rewards—
for instance, the prospect of raining
on rude tourists

a weather of coleslaw & fried shrimp.
That our cod-
pieces grew more explosive
each day helped us believe

in the mission.
Our sweat-soaked shirts raised,
the waist bands
of our polyester pants pulled down,

we searched for busboy
birthmarks born
of fierce chafing.
With their Teflon

hands the managers might suddenly
slap us—
Those moments where death
felt moments away—

Checking to see
if we'd stick to the training,
not call out the names
of the ones we loved

(our loved ones
who would never understand)
testing to see
if we'd keep busing

like each table was a voice
buried alive. Many questions were served
in the busboy training.
Like: *Could these new faces*

be removed? Could they ever be
cleaned & serviced?
& when finally it seemed
nothing could touch us—

We were wrong,
everything could touch us.
The managers
let us go.

—MEMORIAL DAY—

for the Busboy Coat-of-Arms

You are blazed
in the fried-food tradition.
You are encircled by sizzling

snapping scallops. You unslug
the giant squid from the cave
of you beneath a boozy moon,

amidst a baptism of clams
& burning crab cakes.
Untie with your tongue

the waitress from her apron.
For service shadow
her shadow

like a fuse.
How you hold your breath
through the rich heart of summer

clogged with family
feuds & bad tippers, the cheap
specials & side

"baked" potatoes steamed
in the steamer
since before you were born.

Those black & white checkered
polyester pants you throw
cornstarch down

so your ass won't rash.
Those ceiling fans reeling
with eels

of smoke from the cigarettes
of a thousand tourists
crammed in a single booth.

We should fear for you—
Those constellations
of jagged shells
straining the trash you cart
like a shield,
that tongue of butter

leaking through
trying to lick the soles
of your shoes.

—NAME YOUR POISON—

My eyes lisped like flames
in a headache
THE CLAM SHACK! on my shirt

bleeding a Rorschach
sweat test
(can you read it?)

its inner eclipse
bestubbled & baked
out of bloodshot & baking

because I got busted
checking out Bethany's ass
by the boosters

the buoys & the by-&-by
a bedlam of butter & beer
spilled over

tourists (barbarians)
& managers (barbarians)
big-bellied with battle-axes

to grind
bullshit to your spine
bitch-&-bitch

& those Boston baked beans
a busboy can stand
for only so long

belittled & battered & brain-
bashed out
bewildered & sorrowed

like something beached
waiting for the end
of a shift

—GENERAL ATTRIBUTES—

About a thousand tourists a year
will choke on a busboy
according to the statistics.

*

The mysterious Waitress Triangle
where service disappears.

*

The famous grilled cheese
where the busboy's face emblazons
spontaneous
in buttery heat.

*

The origins of the word
are iffy at best.
It means *nowhere in sight,*
stealing your tips,
seeker of the waitress panties.

*

Your mother was a busboy.

*

Jesus
was a busboy.

*

There have always been two kinds:
the ones who distract you
while you pay your bill
& the ones who find your car
out in the lot
& chew the rubber strips from its
   windows.

*

I thought
if you were a busboy
your future was ominous
as a motel at dusk.
Then I read the legend
where food service workers
battle the economy's
giant squid to a draw.

*

Then
I *became* a busboy.

*

& *married* a waitress.
Just like in the opera.

–DEFINITION–

—NOUN

as in one who sets & assists; Ho Chi Minh & Al Pacino; accidental; as in boxes & tubs not aesthetically pleasing; as in from school this kid you knew that you never really knew; they may wear a black apron, they may wear a white apron; from the Greek *ever yearning for imperfection*; from *guarding against ugly and nowhere in sight*; Langston Hughes, busboy poet; raw dog screaming cannabis; slang for *definitely not doing his job*; slang for *disturbed*; slang for *urinating in public*; the blackest white-boy ever apoplectic; as in from school this kid you knew that you never really knew, he was actually called *The Busboy*; training wages, typically minimum, typically needs verification; pornographic **CLAM SHACK**; Studio 54; as in the match lit at Coconut Grove; as in additional duties; as in *I have always told the truth, even when I lied*; this kid you knew that you never really knew, he was actually called *The Busboy*, for his ever yearning, for his imperfection, for the *thousand years before he got laid*.

—FIRST SHIFT—

The busboy about to train me:
smoking pot at the edge of
the dock kept his lessons sharp.

The busboy about to train
me: tying back his glorious
mullet, explained essential
aspects of the busboy matrix.

Like: how to ambush a waitress,
jilt the time clock, keep zip-ties handy,
save your pennies for
that asshole on
the turnpike who rides
your bumper like a clown—a handful
will make a myth of his windshield.

Then a waitress said: *don't be a sucker*, insisting that
the busboy training me had the heart
of a Boy Scout.

But it was true: he *did* have the heart of a
Boy Scout.

He kept it in
a jar in his locker.

—SMOKE BREAK—

: The customers were re-
volting.

: The customers were starting food
fights.

: The customers
were disturbed, making
grenades from rolls & hot butter which
got the idiot assembly of
managers
involved.

: Some customers were
having heart attacks & falling face-
first into baskets of clams.

: Some
needed a good spanking.

: Some customers
were punk ass kids
& some of those kids had
puked in the gift shop where all the mops had gone missing.

: There was a lot of vibrating among customers
& a total
lack of grace.

: There were customers, more
than a few, who
found themselves the object
of a common busboy fantasy, zip-tied & stuffed in
the trunk of a car speeding back
to Massachusetts.

: Then the waitresses decided
to unionize but
the union was busted
by The Garbage Bag of Death.

: & a customer slipped & broke her
hip but not until she complained
first about her meal but
she didn't actually complain about her meal until she'd
licked her plate clean.

: There were reports of a man wandering around with a bow & arrow
a melting popsicle a spork
wearing pink
bunny slippers & Jackie-O
glasses yelling *The End
Is Near!*

          : & the waitresses decided over Lucky Strikes
if they couldn't form a union then maybe they'd start a cult.

: A cult based on the belief that a certain busboy
has been lately stealing
their tips.

: Your name was mentioned.

—INITIATION—

The manager sticking

        his hand in the breading. The manager

   sticking his breaded hand

       in the Frialator *just long enough*

when he pulls it out
a frequent nightmare-looking thing encrusted

       in sudden crust emerges. Then the manager
says to the new busboy

       the new busboy who stands there blinking

horrified not knowing what
the manager
     says

       Don't fuck with me.

** ** ** ** ** **

     But gradually that manager

   will act all friendly
     toward the new busboy

       asking if he remembers

blowing bubbles when he was a kid?
When the new busboy says *Sure*

I remember.
the manager will say *Well he's on the phone now*

asking for you.

—UPSIDE-DOWN CRATES—

I would get these *assertions*
like a bucket of eels. These *serious*
denials like seagulls
screaming in the fog
of your parents' love life. Like the butt-
head tourist kid on the dock pitching

Alka Seltzers to the screaming gulls.
Maybe it was when the chowder cook
said he downshifted
into third & took the dirt road home
on his date with the waitress.
The middle-aged middle school teacher
waitress. The middle-aged waitress

who could have been my middle school
teacher *back in the day*. Who somehow *enjoyed*
waitressing in the summer
which is the opposite of
summer, *in order to keep busy.*

I would be sitting

alone on the upside-
down crates anticipating the uncertainty between
the last party of the night & dragging
my ass back to work
the next morning. Sitting on the upside-down
crates *searching for the meaning*
of sitting on the upside-down

crates considering what
it means for the crates to be upside-down.
Stunned at the possibility
that downshifting
into third with the chowder cook
in the cab of his truck was somehow

a middle school teacher's idea
of keeping busy.

—PINK PILLS—

His eyes kept making
annoying sounds
ever since he took
the funny pink pills.
The new condos
seemingly carved
from seashells—
he climbed one
to the second floor.
Vandals had spray-painted
porn on the walls
but it was good holding
his breath like a knife
in the dark.
Eventually
he'd have a vision—
the waitress cult
in gorilla masks
abducting him to the un-
finished basements.
Tying him to a dirty mattress.
Having their way
through the Civil War
of Memorial Day weekend
leaving him for the builders
to find. Basically
that was the problem
with the pills.
They could make a busboy
sentimental.

—NATIONAL FLAG WEEK—

When the hostess comes
out to apologize
for over-fried clams

she's doing her job—
Apologizing for *disappointing* fried clams.
Apologizing for fried clams that have *underachieved*.

Apologizing for fried clams
that have lost their sense of purpose.
It was determined

the cheese slices stuck to the ceiling
must have had their reasons.
Generally

as they prepped your food
the cooks would listen *unironically*
to 80s speed metal.

The locker room
where socks
had gone to die.

The lobster tank where now & then
a lobster tried to escape,
but the others

would drag him back—
This isn't about the flawed
democracy of lobster tanks,

the sweaty dictatorship
of managers
at the bar with toothpicks

in their mouths
saying things like *You missed a spot.*
Or the unacceptable conditions

the green dumpsters worked under,
wheezing blue fluid
to the bay

where the tourist attractions
were tourists
who were attractions

thanks to their shitty parallel
parking skills.
The new rich estates

along the shore
looked like cheap estates
trying to look

like old rich estates.
On the bulletin board
in English & Spanish were directions

for what to do
if someone was choking.
If you were choking in another

language too bad for you.
Still—
There were times busing tables

when I felt strangely free.
Yet no one asks
how I came to be a busboy.

It was the same way
anyone becomes a busboy.
Someone on the inside

vouched for my character.

—THE TRAINING—

There were *serious fly problems*
out by the dumpsters.

It became
a situation.

The managers
decided to hang jars

with a rainbow liquid inside.
The flies would fly in,

experience a cold
night of reality,

then die.
But not right away.

There was time
for a fantastic fly orgy—

Layers of flies screwing
over layers of flies dying

over layers
of creamy maggots

who were thinking
God-knows-what.

Worse was to picture
smashing those jars,

but the possibility
excited every busboy's thoughts.

In the meantime,
as the jars filled

management explained,
holes would have to be dug—

At least three feet deep.
According

to some ordinance or something.
It was later suggested

that burying the jars
was a metaphysical demonstration—

Like a manager's sense
of humor

or the inevitable failures
of attempting closure.

—PANDEMONIUM DAY—

I didn't *choose*   to smash the windows
the windows   *chose me*
I believe in the casualty   of the vandal's *free will*
I believe *stealing* swigs of milk   straight from the carton
is a form of critique   our shortening spans of attention
will require wisdom to fit   on napkins
it's why fortune cookies   were invented & bathroom
graffiti & why *Saturn*   *Devouring His Children*
should be hanging at the door   of every restaurant

—FATHER'S DAY—

The managers would be planning a new plan.
But before they could plan the new plan in full
they would first have to plan it in half.

But—

Before they could plan the new plan in half
they would first have to plan it in quarters.

& yet—

Before they could plan any new plan in quarters
they would first have to plan those quarters in half.

That was the beauty of management—

—EPIC—

the clam roll

               pissing lemon juice
                      down the French

fries'

               crinkled leg

woke the manager—

               (that's what started the war)

—LYRIC—

From the ass of **THE CLAM SHACK!** I stumbled
to the beach where I figured the stars
for buckshot until I was too stoned to think.
No ride home (*it didn't exist*) I passed out
where the surf could kiss my greasy sneakers.
When I came to, another busboy
was wandering the dunes with a pool cue
trying sink the moon in the corner pocket.

—PICKING UP THE 7-10 SPLIT—

I never met a mascot
that I didn't want to smack

in the giant face. A terrible fact I
live with like how Bibles sleep in

bedside drawers in motels.
My uncle...
the one & only time we met

he said people
could just catch on fire. It's called

spontaneous combustion.
We were at the bar sharing

a pitcher of Schlitz &
a corned-beef.

I was maybe 10 years old. It's what
you call
a *formative experience.*

—FLASHLIGHT—

The man waits
for something to happen.

Not that nothing
is happening.

(It is.)

You can poke your finger through it
like wet paper.

So management says
Hang a dish rack.

—No problem!
Six hours later—

Screwdriver & hammer-
sized holes in the wall
yet the job
remains extremely undone.

So the man reads about a guy
who claims he can build a boat
just by thinking real hard
about building a boat.

Meanwhile
the wall with screwdriver
& hammer-sized holes...

The man suspects
something is happening
there in the wall.

Something *important*.

But to see it he'll need
a flashlight

management hasn't invented.

—TYPEWRITER—

a found poem

QWERTY DOESN'T LIVE HERE ANYMORE
HE FELL OFF THE BRIDGE PLAYING FRISBEE

—PIRATE DAYS—

he kept seeing

the same sets

of fuzzy dots

basically

it was winged goats

mountained

in the dying blue

of a tv

thieved

in the corner

of his dreams

watching him watch

like the logic

   of a watch

it was

the language talking

like

managers sitting

in lifeguard chairs

suspicious

watching him eat

a sandwich

or take a piss

he could deal with that

but one night

the managers

were watching him

watching the goats

watching him

and you think

you

have problems

—THERE'S *TARTAR SAUCE* ON YOUR FACE!—

—STRAIGHT FACE—

The waitress in her grace had agreed
to get naked so I was trying to keep a straight face
but my hands & her neck

where my mouth should have fit deliciously
smelled like fried
food, & as we were at the beach the subject became

for awhile sand
in my crotch & hers, complicating a-mightily
my straight face abilities

& forget
the fog, the usually
perfectly philosophical fog

blowing in not sublimely
across the salt marsh & road smelling
of clams

or the swollen moon, traditionally
confessional, that seemed beer-battered
at best, but the tide, the peripatetic

tide...
Friends, if you must hear the form-
less sizzle of a poem

with everything in it,
work a double
then listen to the tide.

—GROUT—

some are born into groutness   others have groutness thrust upon them
  grout zero

```
a
l                            g           no grout about it
l                            r
                             o
a     the grout depression   u
l                            t           grout grout damn spot!
o
n        t                   s                persona non grouta
g        h                   c
         e                   o
t                            t                          g
h        g                   t                          r
e        r                                              o
         o     i'm the groutest                         u
grout          u                                        t
r        t          grouting thomas                    c
                                                        h
o                                                       o
u        g                                              m
t        a                                              a
         t     "grout" a little louder now             r
t        s                                              x
o        b          "grout" a little louder now
w        y
e                        "grout" a little louder now
r
```

```
                                    g
                    grout scott!    r
            the grout American dream o
                                    u                                    r
Alexander the Grout                 t       Ulysses S. Grout             e
                        t                                                s
                        h           t                                    t
            g           e           i       little miss groutshine       l
            r                       t                                    e
            o           g           s                                    s
G           u           reports of my grout have been greatly exaggerated s
r           t           o
o                       u                                                g
u           e           t               the grouts of wrath             r
t           n                                                           r
```

—POSTMODERN T-SHIRTS—

In our city there was a martini-shaped building
called the Hansen

Building. Basically: the waitress
who bought the busboy's bullshit

believed the Hansen Building was named
for the band Hanson.

There were tourists with conflicting
t-shirts. One said:

I fucked the girl from Hanson.
Another said I'm With Stupid.

There was no resolution.
But there was a story

in the form of a baby also wearing
an I'm With Stupid t-shirt

except the arrow on that shirt
pointed straight up

so it meant either the parents were stupid
or God was stupid.

Some of us were partial to the thought that
that made the baby a postmodern baby.

The postmodern baby eating Cheerios
in his postmodern onesie

totally not avoiding confusion
bogging down the pink-haired postmodern

waitress who was still old-fashioned
enough to eat beer nuts & read Moby Dick

on break. She had a tattoo on her shoulder
of a smoking starfish.

I would find myself watching
just to see it move.

But that's nothing.

—FLIP A COIN DAY—

The Wicked Witch thrifts a gift shop
snow cone. The Bionic Woman's
fetching heavy cream.

The busboys break
beats on the dock
with a six-pack of Worst Beer

shouting *Eat Me!* at the river.
Dorothy rigs a sail chair, locks the Wicked
Witch in a restroom the cooks

abuse. There's a motivational
poster over
the toilet

of Aristotle, the only
waiter **THE CLAM SHACK!** has known,
throwing down

a vicious two-handed clam basket on Alexander
the Great back when he was minimum-
waged. The Bionic Woman

fetches heavy cream, begs
a certain question: Can a top-secret management
food service division create a cream

too heavy
for her to lift? The Wicked
Witch spits hexes but Dorothy's like—

Whatever. The horniest busboy of all time says,
I'd screw an eel if I could hold it down
by the ears.

The tide feels low
where rusted shopping
carts appear. The Wicked Witch deals

a swap: Dorothy's scuffed ruby-reds
for a pair of big-girl stilettos. Blur your vision
at the motivational poster
& the first tourist
to moon a crowd emerges. Remember: busboys
make the best forgetters

& when that goody two shoes Dorothy
unrigs the door, the Wicked Witch sails & shivs her
with a snow cone.

The restaurant drags its tired butt, but
never shuts its smack-talk mouth. The tourists pull
up in buses. The truth has gone on strike.

-DISTURBIA-

I'm the latest drub diets
      with my stub dried biter duds!
Check my dusted ribs
         of udder bits rutted in the yard!
Dusting up the bed turds
           my bride stud wears the bigs!

—THE GOLDEN AGE—

for Mike Theune

Managers were always lamenting the olden days
when busboys were interesting & focused,
reliable & self-sufficient.
Like protagonist Marlboro Men—
Idiot smoker's management nostalgia
for when busboys supported the cause & did it all,
were detail oriented
& never so boring as to get drunk & pass out
on the beach with the tide rolling in
without a witness.
Grease fire in the kitchen?
A busboy could organize his breath
& blow it out.
The restaurant a confusion of dirty tables,
a riot of tourists?
One busboy alone could handle it
working double-shifts inside every minute for weeks
at the height of summer, frequently hung over
but his mechanics were always solid,
he was never late.
Never!
The tables would be so clean
you could eat off them.
That's how one manager put it. You used to be able
to EAT off a table when a busboy was done.
Those busboys were punctual.
Those busboys weren't ashamed
of their black & white checkered polyester pants.
But for some reason—it's unclear—
the model busboys of yesteryear hung it up,
their trash bags & orderly ways,
& said fuck this!

The death of The Golden Age of Busboys.
Management has been trying to find them
ever since.
But all that gets hired are punk busboys
who half-ass their way through shifts.

This has been your **CLAM SHACK!** pep talk.

—BASTILLE DAY—

Tourists eating stuffed clams
stuffing themselves
like stuffed clams.

Those polyester pants
scratching your ass like fiberglass.
The fiberglass pants rash

knitting a net.
Trying to scratch it surreptitiously
when you noticed swimming

for the exit
a fried jumbo shrimp.
Its neck (or whatever)—

You thought if you tied a little
cape-napkin around it
with a Superman "S"

or maybe "Ladies Night Out!"
on the cape
then left it trayed

in the waitress station
it would be a gratifying disorder.
Irreverence—

It's always a matter of perspective
& when it turned out
the jumbo shrimp

was actually a turd instead
you had to accept certain truths—
The oxymoron of the jumbo shrimp

that a shrimp-shaped shit
could get flushed
somehow down a tourist's leg.

It was the hottest day of summer
& wrestling in your thoughts
were some important things—

Empathy & focus—
When they "asked" you
to clean it up.

—MYTHIC—

The busboy who slipped
    & fell off the dock

       sat there awhile
          soaking in the bay

             looking up

      at the strange things

      changing

in the clouds. When the gulls
      descended

          one landed on his head.
          It was

      a mythic scene.   People keep
        statues of it now

in their yards.

—A PEOPLE'S HISTORY OF THE UNITED STATES—

My father whistled
at the Bunker Hill Monument,
calling it one hell
of an erection.

My mother looked
extremely unamused.

I was in the back
with a history book,
my legs stuck to the vinyl
like cheese.

But wait. According to this
the Battle of Bunker Hill
actually happened at Breed's Hill.

The car filled with
a stony silence.
The stony silence of the dis-
enfranchised G████s.

An erection...

On Breed's Hill...

It must have been too much
for history to take.

—INDEPENDENCE DAY—

I can picture my mother
after waitressing, forever
     reading the entrails
        of her apron.
    In a hushed voice she says:
I'm halfway through my thirty-day diet
& already I've lost fifteen days.
    In the bleachers
        at the ballgame on TV
someone who looks like
    my father with a mustache
& tan has his arm
        around another woman.
    In a kitchen
six shades of dusk my mother
beautiful & clairvoyant
    burns the fish-sticks
        in a skirt of smoke.
          When my father comes home
      she's holding the lamp
like a hammer. She says
she feels *enlightened.*

—TAKE YOUR PANTS FOR A WALK DAY—

So what that Rilke's psycho mom
dressed him in checkered pants.

So what that he skipped like a restless schoolgirl
& was snubbed

by that chowder-head Tolstoy!
Screw Tolstoy!

When Rilke whipped
his throbbing lobster out

& whispered *presto*
it scared management so bad

they fired him with pay—
Rilke's plan all along.

Nowadays all the busboys
think they're in a band

but can any of them play?
Whereas Rilke could steal a kazoo

from the gift shop
& make it sing like Justice

was sitting on his face.
He invented that song

in his *tumescent* youth.
What I'm saying

is the waitress who inspired Rilke's
words had a loneliness that burned

to the moon & back.

—COURAGE—

What Boy Scouts
        demanding S&M merit badges
    have to do with Huey Lewis

    look-alikes lining up
        along the bar is unclear, but those political flyers
            on the poles out front get along

            with truth
    like urine cakes to urine.
    At least the fake roses

            smell like real smoke. What preachers
            preach Gospels of the Waitress? How many
    Huey Lewis look-alikes

        will line up along the bar? Someone
    makes a joke, says they need a new drug.
        Someone

    half-joking says
  the Huey Lewis look-alikes—
    If we only had their courage.

—ESCAPE ARTIST—

Harry Houdini could escape any
thing. He escaped
the 17th ward. He escaped his name.
Nobody wanted to see
an Erik Weisz
escape from a pair of black & white
checkered polyester pants so he slipped
into Houdini after bootlegging his way
from Hungary, which he called
Appleton, Wisconsin.
That's how good he was—
He was a Hungarian named Erik Weisz
who tricked everyone into thinking he
was a Houdini from Appleton, Wisconsin.
His father was a chowder cook. His mother a colossal
a deep sigh of a wave. Hello?
In school he could make gym disappear.
He was voted Most Likely
To Be First in Line. Then he was voted Most Likely
To Die. At airports he escaped being strip-searched
with swagger. In Russia he escaped from Siberia.
In *Escape from New York* he escaped
from New York with a case
of hundred dollar bills. He could escape
all kinds of shit just by holding his breath. He could even
escape his image in a mirror—as good
as escaping time. Compared to that, being
suspended upside-down in a tank filled
with managers & electric eels
was nothing. He was like
a curtain. He was like a pair of dark shades.

A mouth of gold teeth.
He would regurgitate small keys at parties
to impress chicks. When he had to work in a restaurant
he bused tables with his thoughts. When he kissed
the waitresses he never moved his lips.

—NATIONAL ICE CREAM SANDWICH DAY—

When the busboy slips
like a bride off the dock
his shift shifts
a few degrees of difficulty.

The restaurant needed
a spanking all morning
& would need a good spanking
all summer long.

The novelty slingshots
in the gift shop. Inevitably
a genius loads one up
with something hellish & fried.

When will management
get as serious about syntax
as syntax is serious
about management?

About the philosophical
implications of boiling
lobsters alive?
About the cooks

prepping your meal
in a balloon of speed metal?
A busboy's feet can be
of several minds like a locker

full of Converse All-Stars.
Sometimes it feels
the tourists are vibrating
in your lap.

Then a guy in a powder blue
jump suit strolls in
& orders twenty clam rolls
like clam rolls are part

of the weather.
It's true, when the restaurant
is slamming, a busboy
& waitress are one.

The moon
& a busboy, the beach
& a waitress, and later
maybe karaoke.

—DOG DAYS—

It was so hot
you'd singe your fingertips
opening a car door.

That's nothing compared
to how we did each other.
The mattress shoved

to the center of the sublet.
Cicadas buzzing so loud
they sawed through

our thoughts.
Nothing hidden.
A defining moment,

& that was the problem.
How a thing defined
resists what it means.

When nothing was left
but words to eat
it was because we'd blown

a week's check at the bar.
One of our fantasies
had been to wreck the spinning

rims on the asshole
landlord's truck.
For fun we dragged

a couch to the curb
& watched lightning lose
itself like spare change.

—DOMINOES—

The owner who chewed me out
        with his zipper unzipped
was my favorite. Once during the rush
    I saw him get slapped
by an absurdly
        hot waitress.

With any luck a waitress like that
    would slap me, too.
Meanwhile the cooks were watching

        a domino geek on TV
set up something
    like a gazillion dominos.
They went spiraling
        up a ramp, then the one at the top
jumped through
    a flaming hoop. It was impressive
especially if you imagined
        that domino

    as something stupid you've done
that you can't take back.

—HUMAN RESOURCES—

Finally the copier just jig-sawed & Swiss-cheesed
& otherwise minced & shredded
the new menu specials to a stubble-mulch lettuce…

Something had to be done.

    A waitress distracted the copier with a lobster
while I dialed the emergency number
& whispered the secret word

    _____.

When I hung up
the SWAT Team was already there
rappelling in a shadowy flux
from the roof.

The copier sensed something was up—

It drooled ink & toner from its face.
    Its digital readout reading in tongues

flashing a seizure
of stop & go.

    Debbie, I said—
If that was even the waitress's name—
Take my hand.

Then the SWAT Team swung through
the windows like axes swift
through the haze with their laser scopes trained—

They outflanked the copier quick,
had it blindfolded & unplugged.
The restaurant's CO
lit a cigar while two boys in back
went to work with some pipes.

The CO shook his head.
He had a grim expression.
He said: *We've seen this type of copier before.*

-THE WEEKLY WEEK-

I saw the best minds
of my generation lobster-
bibbed
& buttered,
heard its voices
mushroom-clouded
& bused through
the stew,
then paid five dollars
for the experimental theater
where *The Nativity Scene
Musical* referred
only obliquely
to actual scenes of nativity...

The ominous Madonna
impersonator
impersonating Madonna...

                    The double shifts
that passed sentence
in a sentence
or less.

I saw the words *ladies night*
on a napkin
while on the news some economically

accompliced village
idiots of my generation
intentionally
drilled holes in a wildlife
refuge
as officials dropped like dishes.

I felt the skid
marks of my generation, the marooned
forms, the Miss Teen New Hampshire
& the young woman doomed
to be mauled
by her assumptions
& own fur coat.

I was there for the migrating
salmonella outbreaks
when authorities
hauled in for questioning
the likes of Mr. Peanut.

I could barely distinguish the best
rock operas from the worst,
streams
of incoherent consciousness
conflated with the dangers
of pinball wizardry.

I felt the complex
of feelings of my generation,
layered in on themselves
like onions that deserve better
than what the cooks can give.

I wondered
did size matter.
I wondered what if.
The long questions of my generation
slipping off the short dock of the void. The poison

industries that finally said
Screw it!
& started targeting pets.
The not so much,

the cooked & coughed & cut,
the paradigm
of Mr. Peanut's syntax
in creamy & chunky
forms.
I proposed the awkward
propositions, moved through their motions,

witnessed the best mimes
of my generation
escape
imaginary dodecahedrons in nothing
more than black tights.

The best minds of my generation...
Who kick-assed & verbed
too heavy & fast for their ape bodies.
Too meta-amphetamined.
Who listed like horoscopes, loved
like love to its eye, the I
to its mirror.
Who tried, & we
are with you.

–KISS & MAKE UP–

The busboy who trained me
wasn't always human. Sometimes he was a busboy. Sometimes he was waiting like a fitting room
for something to enter and try on
weird pants. He would explain

there were worse things. Road kill for example.
Someone had to put their boots on,
go out there & scrape it off. I was
biking home from work one night when a bat suddenly

tangled in my spokes. A palpable
argument. Then it was over. Which made perfect sense.
A bat flapping in the plot of a wheel's spokes has no

business lingering in
indecision. The house I lived in
with some other barbarians was like a book left out

in the rain or smoke. When I got there
the chapter where the party's in progress

was already in progress. The busboy who trained me had actually
gone to clown college so sometimes he would turn himself

into a cyclone. At some point he would end up on the lawn making
beauty by spitting fire into the telephone
wires until the cops arrived. There were

coincidences. Talk of the afterlife.
A hostess in a zodiac dress.
She invented

mottos that were little knives
aimed at the restaurant's heart. **THE CLAM SHACK**:
Where No Sorrow Is
Too Big! I remember thinking as night turned into

the sorry mess of morning that the tip
of her cigarette in the dark was the irradiated breath of
an angel. Which is boring. & stupid. But the end
of summer was beginning & I was feeling good.

The busboy who trained me was determined to teach me
one thing or another. It was
a question of degrees. An immensity beneath everything
making tracks in my thoughts, filling me up
with a dumb hope.

—NATIONAL HOT DOG MONTH—

The forces of clock-
work were undermined like clock-
work.

    *

A busboy walks
into a bar—

              An instance
of the instant vibrating
in language.

    *

The restaurant
never asked you to
imagine imaginary
things like the brittle
bones of onion rings.

    *

According to
one busboy's aesthetics
adding *anal*
to the names of SUVs
greatly enhanced
the work.

    *

...The Anal Ex-
plorer, The Anal
Aviator,
The Anal Frontier...

*

Responding
emotionally
confirmed
a hypothesis that the brain

accrues fragments as in
a dream, if he was eating
a clam roll
abducted by tourists
in transit or transition
the busboy basically was mired
in syntax.

*

Clocks would strike thirteen, you'd wake dizzy
in a Hampton Beach ice bath with
your kidneys kidnapped
& a ransom note
lip-sticked to the mirror
was one con-
sequence

*

of experience.

*

The it of the restaurant
grits its teeth.
Its circus & havoc.
A venture that moved
through whatever moved
through you.

*

Kept moving.

*

A busboy could get intro-
spective in the way
a sea anemone
could turn itself inside
out like a pink
umbrella.

*

Sometimes he would wear
the voice of his black & white checkered pants
suspicious of being watched
by the eyes on dollar bills.

A manager could well be
in the back playing
checkers online
getting his ass whipped
possibly by someone named muff
2tuff.

*

One day a guy with *Easy
Rider* tattooed on his face
found a pretext for
ordering off the kids' menu...

...The evidence
was around us
in the margins. It was
marginal evidence.

*

It was important to
remember the consolation
that some turtles live
longer than some
civilizations.

*

There were interventions.
A ticker tape of uncertainty.
Waitress murmurs.

*

There were pills every
busboy tried that
would make the records sound
like the records sound
like they're skipping.

*

From patron saint to patron
sinner at the speed
of takeout.

*

There were certain obstacles—
The chowder cook
who believed in
nothing—Teenybopper
jailbait porno-
graphically sipping
gift shop Slurpees
that glowed weapons grade
plutonium
green—Somebody screaming.

*

Inevitably a busboy
gets tartar sauce on his face.

—THE OTHER SIDE OF SUMMER—

with thanks to Marc McKee

the vast theoretical dividing (of the patriarch-ally prescribing words u were
using, or under using, or unwilling 2 use, like = and & signs 4 the non-
representational, or miss-(spell) I*n*g*s*4 the busboy's voice, etc.) between
what u could do 2 unseat the signifying super-chain of dominance & how
exactly that's supposed 2 ever get the managers 2 listen

−33 BUSBOY PROVERBS (AN EVOLUTIONARY ANALYSIS)−

structures   varieties   contexts   functions
structures   varieties   contexts   functions
structures   varieties   contexts   functions
structures   varieties   contexts   functions
structures   varieties   contexts   functions
structures   varieties   contexts   functions
structures   varieties   contexts   functions
structures   varieties   contexts   functions
structures   varieties   contexts   functions
structures   varieties   contexts   functions
structures   varieties   contexts   functions
structures   varieties   contexts   functions
structures   varieties   contexts   functions
structures   varieties   contexts   functions
structures   varieties   contexts   functions
structures   varieties   contexts   functions
structures   varieties   contexts   functions
structures   varieties   contexts   functions
structures   varieties   contexts   functions
structures   varieties   contexts   functions
structures   varieties   contexts   functions
structures   varieties   contexts   functions
structures   varieties   contexts   functions
structures   varieties   contexts   functions
structures   varieties   contexts   functions
structures   varieties   contexts   functions
structures   varieties   contexts   functions
structures   varieties   contexts   functions
structures   varieties   contexts   functions
structures   varieties   contexts   functions
structures   varieties   contexts   functions
structures   varieties   contexts   functions
structures   varieties   contexts   functions

—ROOKIE—

The chowder cook already shouting

      GET THE FUCK OUT! complicates the kitchen. Arriving to work
in your senseless

      busboy duds, you're the summer money's

            bitch & jester. Those black & white checkered
      polyester pants. That **CLAM SHACK!** logo sweat-

stained past reference. That you'll bus hungover
is rhetorical. Whereas truth soon casts over your limbs
           its net: a mysterious

      rash in a tide of sweat. & in front

of those waitresses, perky as syntax.
      One manager speculates that by shift's end

      probably

you'll be dead. Another says
      says stop being such a wuss, that what you need
        is a haircut & tan. This is the manager

you *like*. She reminds you

         of your grandmother. Whiskey-drunk & surly

        as a bluefish. When she says
      think of busing as a sport
           you picture your trading card's
      vital stats like how much

trash could a busboy bus if a busboy wasn't so bored?
The waitresses chip in, buy

a lobster weighing almost thirty pounds
which makes it older
than management.

Freed off the dock,

it disappears into the bay

the way images float from ideas
the way the green dumpsters compacting trash

are apocalyptic
science fiction & the tourists
freak shows with hunchbacked attitudes
& personalities as contorted
as theories. You & the other busboys convene
the secret meeting in the freezer where the dare
is taped to the door:

ANYONE CAUGHT EATING
LOBSTER WITHOUT PAYING
WILL BE SHOT ON SIGHT. The chowder cook shouting
GET THE FUCK OUT! turns
a new waitress into just another noun in tears. She's been on the job
barely an hour. Now someone will have to tell her
it's all a game, that crying from whatever
the chowder cook says is a typical
& forgivable

rookie mistake.

⊣LABOR DAY⊢

Even clouds
were dirty tables. Tables you could pass
your hands through. The managers wagging tongues,
insisted on having
here-&-now meetings
but they were always postponed
to the there-&-then. The food service gods, or rats
or whatever, took my picture, cut off the head
& stuck it on a peanut butter jar
high behind the line
where the cooks could laugh at it freely.
They called it Fat Baby Head Peanut Butter. Meanwhile
in the parking lot, the lot was parked
with a total lack of grace.
The edge of a word is another word's shadow is the best thing
I ever overheard.
& the advice
of dandelion heads exploding. The terrible whisper of those
polyester pants. On my answering machine for days
would be nothing
but a waitress laughing
like a flowerpot falling
from a ledge.
Fat Baby Head Peanut Butter was fine.
I could live with that. But then someone posted
in the Waitress Station
a missing persons flyer
with my name on it
asking had anyone seen me. There were aliases:
Asshole, Flounder, Snot-Nosed Punk. & the claim
I was known to masturbate *furiously.*
Furiously in all-capital letters—F - U - R - I - O - U - S - L - Y ! —
like there's any other way. One whole wall

in the restaurant
was mirrored. If you paid attention you could actually
see the moment where a busboy
turns away from his image.
A mirrored wall
doesn't prove you exist. But it doesn't prove
you don't.
The waitress whose legs put the yes in my eyes. The small
of her back a four-letter word, so I said so.
It was the beginning of summer's end. I was nothing
& lucky. At the gas station after work
I dropped a quarter in the machine
where a wave of quarters was cresting
impossibly at the edge.

—CLEAN—

There was an octopus in the fish
tank nicknamed Vishnu. There were managers
like lifeguards in their lifeguard chairs watching over
busboys in their busboy wilderness.
There were shadows of customers still
sticking to tables that had
to be unstuck with lemon juice. When a customer
dropped her lobster, time seizured so
I turned to my daydream where
the restaurant wasn't
a superfund site. There was a simple code: you could ignore
the schedule & not punch out for breaks
& take two hour breaks & steal beer from the coolers
& get stoned on the dock

                          AS LONG AS YOU COVERED
FOR EACH OTHER AND KEPT THE DINING ROOM UNDER
CONTROL.

                        & when a busboy was cleaning a table
his hands should resemble a hummingbird's
wings. & when the condiments were being organized
a skilled busboy should spin the ketchup & shakers
like pistols before holstering them in the tray. Only then in the customer's
mind would a table really be clean.